WEEK...

Glasgow

ILLUSTRATED BY
Lucy Davey

pocket mountains

With thanks to Judy, Anna and Eric

Published by
Pocket Mountains Ltd
The Old Church, Annanside,
Moffat DG10 9HB

ISBN: 978-1-907025-617

Text copyright © Nick Drainey 2021
Illustration copyright © Lucy Davey 2021

Printed in Poland

Introduction

Glasgow is the shining example of how a gritty postindustrial port city can achieve a cultural renaissance with its Victorian and art-nouveau architecture a backdrop to an assured cosmopolitanism and an unceasing wave of cultural activities. Once the 'Workshop of the World', with all the glorious built heritage incumbent on such prosperity, it has also achieved fame as a medieval seat of learning and pilgrimage to rival St Andrews or Oxford and as the 'Dear Green Place'. This disputed translation of its earliest name *Glas Cau* today symbolises the proud proliferation of parks and gardens at its heart and all around. Few cities have shown such character and capacity for reinvention and it is this that makes sifting through the layers of its history so compelling for the walker.

Founded in the 6th century by St Mungo, Glasgow gained eminence as an ecclesiastical and scholastic centre from the 12th century – a status that was to last some six centuries. By the 15th century, it had Scotland's second university and largest cathedral after St Andrews. As a trading city, however, Glasgow's credentials were poor. The River Clyde was too shallow even for a medieval port and it was on the wrong coast altogether for trade with Europe and the East.

But by the 1670s the newest and most exciting opportunities for trade were to the West and nowhere was better placed to exploit this – imports of Virginia tobacco and exports of linen to the American colonies were already changing this once sleepy cathedral town's destiny. Though Glaswegians were among the most vehement opponents of the 1707 Union with England, commercially it brought unrestricted access to the colonies and within 60 years there were 300 to 400 ships engaged in American trade here, with merchants controlling a larger share of the American tobacco trade than all other British ports combined.

Downriver the Lower Clyde ports of Greenock and Port Glasgow saw exponential growth, and the deepening of Glasgow Harbour's navigation channel made it one of the world's major ports by the Victorian age. Glasgow's reinvention as the Second City of the Empire was complete.

It was only fitting that such a city should have a built environment to match, and with the powerful Merchants House and Trades House in the vanguard, civic improvements had swept through Glasgow with public squares, boulevards and monumental buildings helping to make it one of the finest of all Victorian cities. The city still retained its green enclaves – the most celebrated today being Glasgow Green, its oldest – as well as creating elegant new spaces such as the West End (Kelvingrove) Park.

Nevertheless, Glaswegians looking to escape the overcrowding and pollution brought by industrialisation began to flock north for the restorative air of the Campsie Fells and other rural retreats. For the new class of landowning merchant there were glorious country estates to retire to. Within the city limits Pollok and Cathkin Braes (part of the Castlemilk Estate) and, further out up the Clyde Valley, Chatelherault, a remnant of one of Scotland's greatest lost treasures, are all now country parks.

The family-friendly walks in this volume explore the best green places around Glasgow, with all routes less than an hour's journey away. Though, like the Victorians, many routes head for Glasgow's open spaces, there are also those that cut through the heart of the city whether by way of its medieval and Victorian architecture, along the Firth of Clyde and the echoes of its proud shipbuilding heritage or past the city's murals that confirm Glasgow's reputation for the arts, as the home of the most original of Victorian architects Alexander 'Greek' Thomson, as well as Charles Rennie Mackintosh, known the world over for his ground-breaking modernist designs.

At every turn history is found – whether at Tinto Hill near Lanark, with its Bronze Age cairn, the Forth & Clyde Canal, where little Clyde Puffer steamships plied their way out to sea, the Greenock Cut, which helped power sugar refineries, cottonmills and iron works in the town below, or the mills below the Falls of Clyde, where Robert Owen introduced progressive practices that would transform the face of work and education the world over. Marching further back in time, the Roman empire's northwestern frontier,

the Antonine Wall, still leaves its footprint across the country here.

Exhilarating high-level walks in the Campsies cast a reflective eye both over the city and the multitude of peaks ranged spectacularly across the Loch Lomond & the Trossachs National Park to the north while strolls in Balloch Castle Country Park and up the volcanic plug of Duncryne offer picture-postcard views of the loch, the national park's centrepiece.

Be aware that exploring sites beyond the city streets involves responsibilities for the walker. This includes keeping dogs on a lead near livestock, sticking to paths to avoid disturbing habitats, showing consideration near private residences and observing diversions, common in forestry and near water.

On some of the shorter routes a map is not necessary, but an Ordnance Survey (OS) map can be invaluable on longer or hill routes, as well as the ability to use one with a compass: the sketch maps in the book are intended to provide rough guidance only.

Glasgow: Weekend Walks

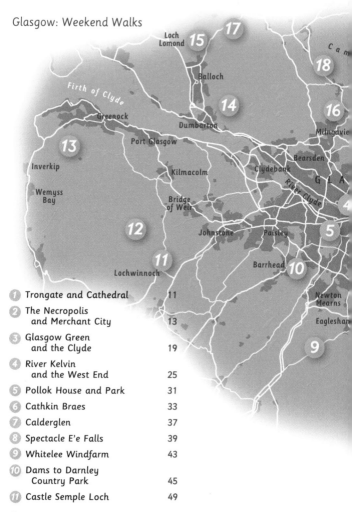

Contents

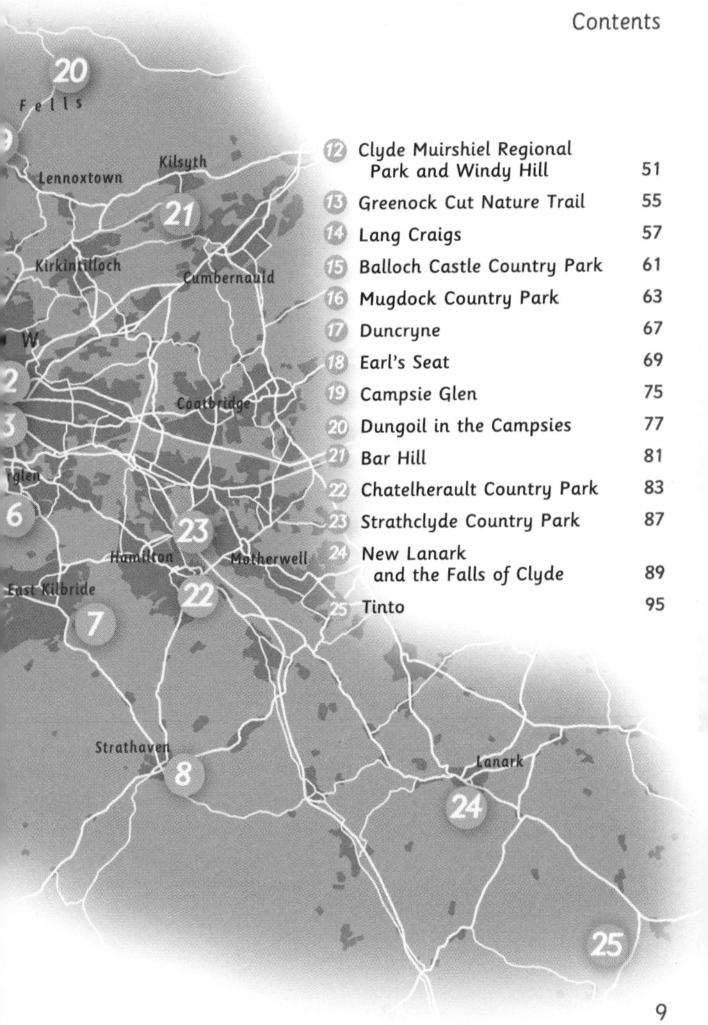

20
Fells
Kilsyth
Lennoxtown
21
Kirkintilloch
Cumbernauld
W
2
Coatbridge
3
6
23
Hamilton
Motherwell
East Kilbride
22
7
Strathaven
8
Lanark
24
25

Trongate and Cathedral

Distance **1.5km** Time **45 minutes (one way)** Terrain **pavements** Access **regular buses and trains to the city centre**

Though today associated with its industrial golden age, Glasgow's history extends back to the 6th century when St Mungo ministered a mile from the banks of the Clyde before building a church where the cathedral now stands. This site, where the city originated, marks the final objective in a walk along part of the Medieval City Trail.

The walk begins at the West Port of the medieval burgh, where Argyle Street's pedestrianised section culminates at Trongate. This would have been a major entry point after being moved here as the city outgrew the West Port's earlier location by the late 16th century. Head down Trongate where in the 18th century Tobacco Lords from the few families that monopolised the trade came to posture. Before you cross Candleriggs, look back to the façade above the amusement arcade, part of a building billed as the world's oldest surviving music hall. Opened in the 1850s, the Britannia Panopticon played host to some of the country's greatest showmen in an area crammed with drinking dens, waxworks and penny theatre, giving a 16-year-old Stan Laurel his first break in the early 1900s.

Ahead is the Tron Steeple. The kirk was razed during over-zealous revelling by Glasgow's ill-famed Hellfire Club in 1793, but the steeple survived and is now a landmark. Beyond this is Glasgow Cross and the Tolbooth Steeple. Marooned mid-road, this is all that remains of the 1626 Tolbooth which held courtrooms, city chambers and prison houses. A long-established gathering place, angry citizens burned the Treaty of Union here before storming the Tolbooth in 1706.

Follow High Street, the 'spine' of medieval Glasgow, up onto Castle Street. Just before the red sandstone Barony Hall, you pass the unsigned Rottenrow, once a fashionable promenade for the canons and clergy.

Famous residents included author Thomas de Quincey in 1846, explorer Dr David Livingstone and Tron Church preacher, Dr Thomas Chalmers.

Beyond this, Castle Street leads into Glasgow's original ecclesiastical heart. Built in 1471 as a manse, Provand's Lordship on the left is Glasgow's oldest surviving medieval house. Opposite is the St Mungo Museum of Religious Life and Art, site of the Bishop's Castle and medieval powerbase. From here continue to the Cathedral Precinct, where the city's first church was built by St Kentigern (St Mungo) – his tomb is here. A cathedral was built in the early 12th century, and the settlement around it was established as a burgh of barony around 1180. The present cathedral, dating from the 13th century, is one of Scotland's few medieval churches to have survived the Reformation intact. Look for the lampposts which incorporate the four symbols on Glasgow's coat of arms, derived from several legends about St Mungo – the tree that never grew, the bird that never flew, the fish that never swam and the bell that never rang. The Necropolis is reached along the cobbled lane over the now covered Molendinar Burn where St Mungo is said to have fished for salmon – the burn was a vital water supply for the medieval town and mills that sprung up along its banks. Return to the start on foot or by bus.

The Necropolis and Merchant City

Distance 4.25km **Time** 2 hours 15 **Terrain** pavements, surfaced paths, steps **Access** regular buses and trains to the centre of Glasgow

The hilltop Necropolis above Glasgow Cathedral is combined in this tour with Merchant City, one-time hub of the tobacco, tea and sugar traders whose names grace the sculptures and monuments of Scotland's most spectacular Victorian garden cemetery.

Scotland's own ornamental 'Père Lachaise' with its 3500 monuments to 'the great and the good' of the Empire's Second City is an enduring reminder of the 19th-century passion for displaying power through architecture. Below it lies Merchant City, administrative and commercial centre for the wealthy tobacco barons and traders of the time and now a regenerated high-end bar and retail area.

Begin the walk at George Square, its entire east side occupied by the monumental City Chambers, which were inaugurated by Queen Victoria in 1888. Head to the left of this edifice to follow George Street for 600m, passing some of the murals that brighten the city's buildings and gable ends, including a *Wonderwall* of Glaswegian innovators at the University of Strathclyde. At the junction with High Street, go left to soon pass Barony Hall, now a university building but one of the best known of the churches for which Glasgow was famous in the 19th century. Looking back is a much-loved gable-end mural depicting St Mungo in the modern day. Just beyond the Barony, cross the road to skirt to the right of the St Mungo Museum of Religious Life and Art, then left at a statue of James Arthur, the Paisley draper who co-founded House of Fraser.

Glasgow Cathedral is directly ahead, but for the Necropolis go right to pass

13

Cathedral
St Mungo Museum
Provand's Lordship
George Square
Hutcheson's Hall
Gallery of Modern Art
George Street
Ingram Street
Glasgow Necropolis
Cathedral Square
Duke Street
Candleriggs
High Street
Trongate
River Clyde
N
500m

through the cast-iron Edington Gates that feature a clipper cresting the globe, symbol of the influential Merchants House which campaigned for the rights and privileges of its members and founded the Necropolis for their benefit – the clipper also rides the rooftop dome of Merchants House in George Square.

A cobbled lane leads across the evocative Bridge of Sighs – turn left after this and climb uphill, ignoring narrow paths peeling off to either side, to reach a fork. Go right here, swinging round for an elevated view of the cathedral. As the wide path starts to veer left, take the steps to the left to a large statue to John Knox, built in 1825, nearly 280 years after the theologian first preached the doctrines of the Reformation here. Return to the main path and drop down past a monument to William McGavin, an often controversial Protestant campaigner. Beyond this is the elaborate temple of the Monteath Mausoleum, built for Major Archibald Douglas Monteath, an officer with the East India Company who died in 1842.

Return to the William McGavin monument and turn left down a path, then left at the bottom to the Bridge of Sighs. Retrace your steps down High Street past the junction with George Street to cross and turn right into Merchant City's Ingram Street. After 200m, just beyond a mural depicting

15

Fellow Glasgow Residents, turn down the historic Candleriggs. After the great fire of 1652, which is thought to have consumed as much as a third of the city, Glasgow's candle factories were removed from the city centre and this street was formally laid out during the 1720s. This end housed an old candleworks while it is believed that Scotland's first sugarworks was further down at Bell Street. Between them was the bazaar founded in 1817 and, later, the 1841 City Halls, Glasgow's oldest purpose-built performance space which in its Victorian heyday hosted greats from novelist Charles Dickens to violin virtuoso Niccolò Paganini. It was also here that author Harriet Beecher Stowe made a plea for the abolition of slavery to a city whose wealth for more than a century had been founded on transatlantic trade in industries that were largely dependent on slaves.

Take the first right to encounter the old Sheriff Court whose elevated portico presides over Wilson Street. The site housed the Merchants House from 1843 before it moved to George Square.

Walk halfway up the far side of the building to view the elegant white face of Hutchesons' Hall, once a hospital for the elderly and a school for the poor, with a glimpse of the arches that connect the City Chambers with their east wing to its left. Nip left down Garth Street to appreciate the opulent Trades Hall, Robert Adam's last project before his death in 1792.

Turn your back on the Italian Centre, with its statue of Italia symbolising the 1990s' regeneration of Merchant City, and go left down Glassford Street to cross at the traffic lights. Carry on along Wilson Street to reach Virginia Street, named after the long-gone Virginia Mansion, built by prominent tobacco merchant George Buchanan and later home of Alexander Speirs whose family was pre-eminent in the tobacco trade. Cross this road, turn briefly left, then duck right along Virginia Court to Miller Street. Turn right here, by the area's last surviving tobacco merchant's house. At the top, go left onto Ingram Street to GoMA (the Gallery of Modern Art), its statue of the Duke of Wellington crowned with a traffic cone. Turn right back to George Square.

Glasgow Green and the Clyde

Distance 8.5km **Time** 3 hours 45
Terrain pavements, surfaced paths,
steps **Access** regular buses to
London Road (250m to start of
walk) from Glasgow city centre

**The heavy industry which
made the River Clyde famous
around the world has all but
gone, but symbols of Glasgow's
shipbuilding heritage can still be
found alongside the waterfront's
shinier, more modern face.**

The 2014 Commonwealth Games did
much to build on the regeneration of
the riverside and this walk west from
Glasgow Green, the city's oldest public
park, is almost entirely traffic free.
Glasgow Green's 55 hectares were
granted by James II to Bishop William
Turnbull who gifted it to the people of
Glasgow in 1450 for grazing, washing,
drying, bleaching linen and swimming.
It was still in use as a drying green
until the late 1970s.

Begin at the Doulton Fountain, a
lavish terracotta symbol of British
imperialism, which was moved to
its present location in 1890 from
Kelvingrove Park, where it had been
built for the International Exhibition of
1888. Across the green you'll see the
distinctive former Templeton's Carpet
Factory which had a chequered early
history. Designed by William Leiper to
echo Venice's Doge's Palace in order to
quell objections from city planners, its
façade collapsed during construction in
1889, killing 29 women in the adjacent
weaving sheds. The factory was finally
completed in 1892.

From the fountain, head to the
right of the French Renaissance-style
People's Palace, opened in 1898 by
the Earl of Rosebery as a cultural
centre. After passing the Winter
Gardens, go through some gates
and turn right past the Nelson
Monument of 1806, the oldest civic
monument to the admiral in Britain
and three decades older than
London's Nelson's Column.

Beyond here a tree-lined drive leads to the McLennan Arch, built in 1792 for the Assembly Rooms on Ingram Street but moved to Monteith Row when the building was demolished a century later. It was moved again in 1922 and finally arrived at its current site in 1991.

Go through the arch, turn left and cross the road (just before it becomes Albert Bridge) to follow Clyde Street along the waterside to Victoria Bridge. Cross the road but not the bridge and drop down to a riverside path leading to the Clyde Arc (better known as the Squinty Bridge due to the angle at which it crosses the river) after 2km.

Cross a road and continue past the dome of the Hydro arena with its translucent cushioned façade and the SEC Armadillo, representing a series of interlocking ship hulls, on the site of the former Queen's Dock. You'll also find the Finnieston Crane here, one of the largest cantilever cranes to have served the Clyde during its industrial golden age.

A path continues by the waterfront to the pedestrian Millennium Bridge. Crossing this, look downriver to the right for the iconic jagged roofline of the Riverside (Transport) Museum. It occupies the site of the shipyard of A & J Inglis which built more than 500 ships, including the *Royal Yacht Alexandra* in 1908 and the *P S Waverley* in 1946. Here, *Glenlee*, also known as The Tall Ship, is permanently berthed, one of just five Clydebuilt steel sailing ships still afloat in the world.

On the other side of the bridge is the Science Centre, and its 127m tower, which sits on the former Plantation Quay, named after the estate bought and renamed in 1783 by a Glasgow banker who owned cotton and sugar plantations in the West Indies.

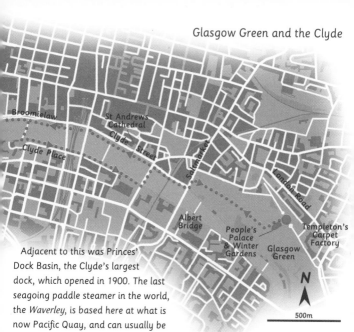

Adjacent to this was Princes' Dock Basin, the Clyde's largest dock, which opened in 1900. The last seagoing paddle steamer in the world, the *Waverley*, is based here at what is now Pacific Quay, and can usually be seen in the winter months.

This whole area was the site of the 1988 Garden Festival held over five months on the centenary of Glasgow's first International Exhibition and featuring acres of greenery, curiosities, tramlines, a rollercoaster and a hint of the more futuristic waterfront to come. Turn left to pass the BBC Scotland HQ before returning over the river on the partially cable-stayed pedestrian Bell's Bridge, which was

constructed for the Garden Festival.

Retrace your steps along the river to the flowing S-shaped pedestrian Tradeston Bridge, also known as the Squiggly Bridge. Cross the river here and carry on along the south bank. After passing the brutalist Glasgow Sheriff Court building, which in 2014 became the first post-war courtroom to gain listed status in Scotland, cross Victoria Bridge and retrace your steps to the start.

4

River Kelvin and the West End

Distance **6.25km** Time **2 hours 30
minutes** Terrain **surfaced paths, pavements,
steps** Access **regular buses to
Kelvingrove Art Gallery and
Museum from Glasgow city centre**

**The Kelvin is a tranquil river
with the sylvan stretch between
the green spaces of Kelvingrove
and the Botanic Gardens in
Glasgow's vibrant West End
home to a variety of wildlife.**

To experience this green tree-lined
corridor, make for the front of
Kelvingrove Art Gallery and Museum,
one of the city's most stunning
buildings, completed in 1901 with
profits from the 1888 International
Exhibition and public subscription.
Incorporating a variety of styles, the
red sandstone edifice is best described
as Spanish Baroque; its two principal
towers are inspired by the pilgrimage
cathedral of Santiago de Compostela.

As well as a renowned art collection,
with a section dedicated to Charles
Rennie Mackintosh, it has a natural
history section with stuffed exotic
animals that have been here since
the museum's inception, including Sir
Roger, a touring 'Menagerie' elephant
who ended his days in Glasgow's
Scottish Zoo. Entry is free and it is
worth timing a visit with the organ
recital held daily in the central hall.

Begin at the main entrance beneath
the imposing statue of St Mungo,
patron saint of Glasgow. Head right,
cross the access road and continue
along the pavement to the Kelvin
Way. The bridge by the same name,
with its symbolic groups of bronze
sculptures, is on your left, but this
route cuts straight across the road
into Kelvingrove Park.

A classic Victorian park, it was
designed by Joseph Paxton, the head
gardener at Chatsworth House.
A terrace curves around the wooded
hilltop ahead, part of the planned
development created in the 1850s
along similar lines to Edinburgh's

Georgian New Town with one of the city's most prestigious addresses, Park Circus, as its centrepiece; the towers of Trinity House and the iconic white spire of Park Church can be seen here.

Take the first path on the left, past the skatepark where Kelvingrove House, later the city's first public museum, stood. It was demolished before the 1901 International Exhibition and the area was given over to an elaborate Venetian Gothic-style Grand Concert Hall, one of the most impressive (if acoustically ineffectual) of the temporary buildings that the exhibition comprised. Over to the east is the ornate 1872 Stewart Memorial Fountain, designed with figures from Sir Walter Scott's *The Lady of the Lake* to celebrate the role of Robert Stewart, Lord Provost of Glasgow, in creating the city's first permanent fresh water supply, from Loch Katrine in the Trossachs, where Scott's poem is set.

Pass the end of the 1895 Prince of Wales Bridge and drop left to continue upstream. As the path rises, turn left below a roadbridge and carry on along the waterside. Cross the next bridge and on the other side turn right to pass below Kelvinbridge, properly known as the Great Western Bridge. After walking under the airy Belmont Bridge, cross the river at Flint Mill Bridge and go left to pass the remains of the eponymous 19th-century mill. The path runs along the mill lade, then through a tunnel below Queen Margaret Drive. Cross the river 130m beyond this via the Humpback Bridge.

Turn right on the other side, then immediately left up steps to Glasgow Botanic Gardens. Go right at the toilets to walk round the magnificent glasshouse of Kibble Palace, conceived in the 1860s by John Kibble (an entrepreneur who also built a horse-drawn camera and a bicycle on floats) and transported by barge from his home on Loch Long to Glasgow.

To visit some of the most elegant terraces in the West End, exit the gardens by the small gate onto Great Western Road. Turn right to pass Kirklee Terrace above you on the right, a Renaissance-style palazzo designed in 1864. Cross Great Western Road at the traffic lights and continue right to reach the magnificent Great Western Terrace. Designed by Alexander 'Greek' Thomson in 1867 and set back from the main road, former residents included Robert Blackie, publisher, and Sir William Burrell, shipping magnate and art collector. Return via the series of terraces parallel to the main road to reach the principal gates to the gardens at the intersection with Byres Road.

Cross here and follow Great Western Road for 700m to Kelvinbridge, taking the steps to the right to rejoin the river. Turn right and return to the Prince of Wales Bridge, now crossing before taking the first left to follow the river past the city's oldest surviving bandstand (1924). Cross the road just before it becomes the Kelvin Way Bridge and follow a riverside path, keeping left at a series of junctions. Cross at the traffic-free Snowbridge, with a view here up to the Gothic revival building that was designed as the fashionable new home of the University of Glasgow in 1870; in scale second only to the Houses of Parliament at the time. Its style and choice of architect – the English George Gilbert Scott – was not without controversy in a city replete with renowned architects. From here, return to the start.

27

Pollok House and Park

Distance **4km** Time **1 hour 15**
Terrain **surfaced paths and tracks**
Map **OS Explorer 342**
Access **regular buses to the park's
main entrance on Pollokshaws
Road (1.5km to start of walk)
from Glasgow; trains to
Pollokshaws West from Glasgow**

**Pollok Country Park is the
only country park within the
city limits yet it feels completely
sealed off from any urban
influences. Woodland, riverside
and wide open spaces make for
a wonderful varied walk through
a landscape that changes with
the seasons.**

The park is part of the Old Pollok
estate, ancestral home of the Maxwell
family for seven centuries until it was
gifted to the city in 1966. Pollok
House itself was built in 1752 as a
stately home for the Maxwells, who
were patrons of art and learning,
and it forms the centrepiece of a
nationally important designed
landscape as well as being the

birthplace of the National Trust for
Scotland when, in 1931, a group led
by Sr John Stirling-Maxwell came up
with the idea for such a body.

Start at the house, facing White Cart
Water, and go left to follow the river
to the estate's stables, passing but not
crossing an elegant stone bridge
designed by William and John Adam
in the 1750s.

The straightforward route is to pass
to the right side of the stables, but
a diversion implemented during
a long-term renovation provides a
worthwhile detour (whether the
diversion is in place or not). Take a
cobbled lane on the left and follow it
round to the right, then turn right to
reach the formal gardens. At the
bottom of these, continue through a
gate to pass the stables on your right.

These stables were once the working
centre of the estate, which can trace
its history to the 12th century when
King David I granted land to Alan
Fitz-Walter, High Steward of Scotland.
The lands were ultimately divided into
Upper and Nether Pollok with the

Pollocks staying on the upper part while the lower section was chartered to the Maxwells, who had first lived here in 1269.

On reaching a track go left and pass a wildlife garden before continuing by the river, going right onto a surfaced path when the track bends left. After a cricket ground and tennis courts the path joins an access road; follow this to the left for 90m before turning right onto a surfaced path.

Cross another access road, then turn right after 80m. If you carried straight on at this point you would arrive at the Burrell Collection, home to

thousands of works of art given to Glasgow by Sir William Burrell and his wife, Constance, Lady Burrell, in 1944. However, your wide path bears left to a junction, where you go straight ahead. At a fork at the top of a hill, go right and then straight on to reach a pond. You are now in North Wood, which contains the largest swathe of old woodland on the estate, in existence since 1741 with a number of veteran oaks and beeches.

Keep left before turning left to walk down a wide surfaced path. Follow the main path all the way back to Pollok House, ignoring any turnings.

6

Cathkin Braes

Distance **3.5km** Time **1 hour 30**
Terrain **surfaced and unsurfaced
paths, muddy in places**
Map **OS Explorer 342**
Access **regular buses to
Carmunnock (1.3km to start of
walk) from Glasgow**

**Cathkin Braes offer grandstand
views over Glasgow, and the
historic and accessible country
park that envelops the hill range
is understandably popular with
walkers. It is also favoured by
mountain bikers and was used
as a venue for the sport during
the 2014 Commonwealth Games.
With 199 hectares and dedicated
walking and cycling trails, there
is plenty of room for both.**

The walk starts from a large car
park on Cathkin Road, 2.5km west of
Cathkin and 1km east of Carmunnock.
From a sign opposite the car park
entrance go down a surfaced path
across grassland, home to the
increasingly rare skylark, whose song
may be heard in summer.

At another signpost on the edge of
Big Wood (ahead of you) take a sharp
turning to the right and follow the
edge of the wood. This woodland
dates back to the 18th century and is
a carpet of bluebells in late spring
when it is also filled with birdsong and
the distinctive drilling of the great
spotted woodpecker. At a carved
wooden bench after 500m, go left into
the trees. Cross a muddy path, turning
right at the next junction to take a
straight line onwards through a stand
of beech trees. Beyond this you can
detour left for a panoramic view of the
city (but watch out for the adjacent
mountain bike trail).

The main route goes uphill after the
beech trees and bears right. As you
lose height slightly, continue in the
same direction, over a mountain bike
trail. After swinging left, you come to
a junction where you turn right to
reach a radio mast and trig point.
At 192m this is the highest point in
Glasgow and the view is stunning,
with the city laid out before you and
the Kilpatrick Hills and Campsie Fells

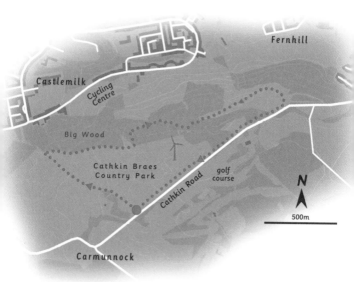

beyond. The area at the top of the braes is known as Queen Mary's Seat for it is believed that in May 1558 Mary, Queen of Scots watched the defeat of her army at the Battle of Langside from here.

Follow the edge of an area of grass to the right, then take the second surfaced path on the right (10m before a metal gate) into woodland. Keep left at all junctions to reach a large wind turbine. This 125m-high monolith was built ahead of the Commonwealth Games and was championed as a new landmark for the city. Carry straight on here, parallel with Cathkin Road which runs back through the grasslands. In summer more than 100 different wildflowers, including white burnet-saxifrage and bright mountain pansy, can be found here, attracting a variety of butterflies, moths and bees. The road leads you back to the start.

34

7

Calderglen

Distance **4km** Time **1 hour 15**
Terrain **surfaced paths and tracks,
steps** Map **OS Explorer 334**
Access **regular buses to Greenhills
Road, East Kilbride (1.5km to start
of the walk) from East Kilbride
and Hamilton**

**Calderglen Country Park, on
the edge of East Kilbride, is
an all-singing, all-dancing
family destination with a huge
playpark, zoo and café. The
trails ranged around the park
are equally impressive and
allow you to leave the crowds
behind as you wander by the
riverbank down into a tree-
lined gorge and through
enchanting woodland.**

This is a good route at any time of
year, from spring and early summer
when the woodland flowers are in
bloom to autumn when the trees put on
their most vibrant display, while a crisp
winter's day of frosted branches,
hedgerows and grass is just magical.

At the top of the main drive into the
country park, go left immediately
after a playground to then swing
round on the path to the right,
passing the private Torrance House,
built as a towerhouse in the 17th
century and later extended.

On reaching a junction at the
bottom of a brief slope go right to
follow a trail high above the Rotten
Calder river which is formed by the
Rotten Burn flowing into the Calder
Water upstream. ('Rotten' means
'red', referring to the colour of the
ironstone over which the burn flows.)
After 550m go left at a junction to
drop down and cross South Bridge.
On the other side take the steps up to
the left and go left at the top to return
along the riverbank to another bridge.
Cross and look at the small weir
below, its shape giving it the name
Horseshoe Falls.

Go right on the other side to follow
the river downstream, ignoring steps
and a path to the left and keeping an
eye out along the water's edge for the
flash of grey wagtails and dippers as
they flit from rock to rock. After

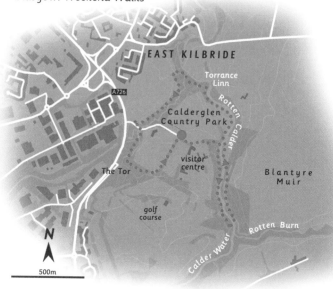

curving left, pass a couple of small waterfalls – Torrance Linn – before taking the steps down to the right. At the bottom shadow the river for 50m, then turn left uphill. Keep right at a junction before dropping down to a footbridge over the Kelvin Burn. More steps follow and at the top an obvious path takes you left alongside a field to turn left, then drop down to the right.

This path leads up to the bridge at the start of the country park's main drive. Cross this bridge and follow a path through woodland to the right on the other side. After 200m a yellow arrow pointing right indicates the site of a Tor or burial mound dating back to the Dark Ages. The main path goes past the yellow arrow and turns left to pass a rugby pitch. Follow the trail left after 150m to return to the start of the walk in the centre of the park with its many attractions.

8

Spectacle E'e Falls

Distance **5.5km** Time **1 hour 45**
Terrain **pavements, field edges,
paths, minor roads, steps**
Map **OS Explorer 335**
Access **regular buses to Strathaven
from East Kilbride and Hamilton**

**Hidden among the rolling
fields of Lanarkshire to the
south of Glasgow are a number
of secluded destinations that
are best experienced on foot.
One such place is the Spectacle
E'e Falls, outside the market
town of Strathaven.**

Only visible when you are right next
to them, the falls in the Kype Water
tumble alongside the ruins of a mill
with an equally dramatic history. The
walk is popular with locals and gives a
good overview of the gentle farmland
that surrounds it.

Start at the south end of Common
Green, the shopping street in the
centre of Strathaven, and go up a
narrow close curiously named Main
Street. Cross a busier road to follow
Todshill Street. Over to the left as you

cross you can spy the remaining tower
of the medieval Strathaven or
Avondale Castle where, according to
one grisly legend, the wife of a long-
past owner was walled up for
displeasing her husband.

Soon after the Drumclog Inn there is
another road junction where you go
straight on to leave town. Some 200m
after a national speed limit sign, go
left over a waymarked stile to skirt
along the right-hand side of a field.
At the other end, go through a kissing
gate to take a trail down to a long
footbridge over the Avon Water. Cross
this and turn right along a path for
50m before bearing left alongside the
Kype Water.

Ignore a little bridge over the burn
and continue to some steps; after
going up these the path swings left.
Turn right at this point to see the ruins
of a mill and the picturesque Spectacle
E'e Falls beyond. Here, the woodland
is home to dipper and kingfisher, while
otters can sometimes be spotted
below the falls at dawn and dusk.

It is said the falls are named after an

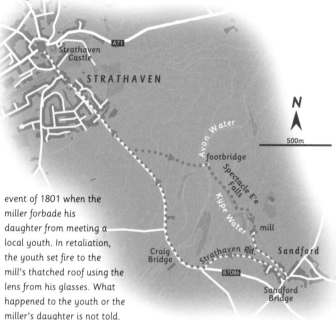

event of 1801 when the miller forbade his daughter from meeting a local youth. In retaliation, the youth set fire to the mill's thatched roof using the lens from his glasses. What happened to the youth or the miller's daughter is not told.

The route continues up more steps and bends left, passing a series of falls. Once over a small footbridge go through a wooden gate and keep to the right side of a field. Cross a stile next to a gate and turn right to walk down a track and past a stone house. The track swings left and becomes a road as it enters the village of Sandford. Turn right at the end to cross a little roadbridge and right again on the other side.

After leaving the village, the road becomes more of a track as it sweeps down to the left and emerges on the B7086. Turn right to follow the pavement for 1.7km, passing Strathaven Ales' brewery and crossing the Avon Water, before returning to town.

9

Whitelee Windfarm

Distance **8km** Time **2 hours 30**
Terrain **surfaced tracks and paths**
Map **OS Explorer 334**
Access **regular buses to Eaglesham
(5.5km to start of walk) from East
Kilbride and Govanhill**

**The largest onshore windfarm in
the UK may not sound the most
obvious of settings for a scenic
stroll but moorland Whitelee,
outside the village of Eaglesham,
is strangely beguiling.**

The whoosh and swoop of the 215
turbines at first seems out of place in
such a remote moorland landscape,
but without them none of the tracks or
paths would be here; instead, this
would be an inhospitable area of
blanket bog and soft ground entirely
bypassed by walkers. The windfarm is
in itself worth the visit – the turbines
are fascinating and there is a good
visitor centre with an interactive
exhibition and café (check times). The
views are the star attraction, however,
stretching to Ailsa Craig and the Isle
of Arran in the Firth of Clyde.

Leave the visitor centre to walk
across the car park and down to a
turbine blade lying on the ground.
Go right just before the blade, past
an information board and through
a gate. Each of the turbines is
numbered, and the track leads to the
first of these (number 40) and then a
junction, where you go left. At the
next junction go right onto a surfaced
path which leads past mountain bike
trails and shelters to a track, where
you now turn left. There is a dedicated
skills loop, pump track and other MTB
trails, but be aware that cyclists may
also use many of the paths and tracks
around the windfarm.

Keep right at the junction before
turbine number 54, then left at a
signpost to gain your first view of
Lochgoin Reservoir. Go right to stay
high above the water and follow a
track up to a signpost, where you turn
left along a trail to a viewpoint on
Blackwood Hill. From the viewfinder
look beyond the turbines to pick out
the landmarks in the Firth of Clyde, as
well as the Trossachs and even as far

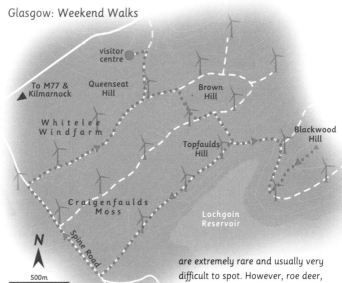

east as the Pentland Hills on a clear day. Retrace your steps to the junction before the point where you had your first view of the reservoir and this time go straight on, following a sign for the Spine Road.

Despite generating enough electricity to power more than a quarter of a million homes, Whitelee is a haven for wildlife. Children are often intrigued by the picture of an adder on a noticeboard at the start of the walk; the reality is that these snakes

are extremely rare and usually very difficult to spot. However, roe deer, brown hare and even otters make this their home. Curlews can be seen and heard, along with wheatears and red grouse, while short-eared owls may be spotted hunting during the day.

When you meet the Spine Road go right and follow it for 900m, past a metal gate on the right and then up to another metal gate on the same side, 30m before a barrier. Turn right here, through the gate and onto a track which leads back to the junction at turbine number 40. Here, turn left to return to the visitor centre.

10

Dams to Darnley Country Park

Distance **8km** Time **2 hours 30**
Terrain **surfaced and unsurfaced
paths, pavement, steps**
Map **OS Explorer 342**
Access **regular buses to Oakbank
Drive (1.2km to start of walk)
from Glasgow and Paisley**

**One of the newest of Scotland's
many country parks, Dams to
Darnley has an excellent path
network, perfect for a watery
wander by large reservoirs that
are home to wildfowl.**

The park covers a total of 546
hectares of greenbelt on the border
between East Renfrewshire and
Glasgow City Council and contains a
glorious mix of wood and grassland,
set amidst rolling fields, making it a
peaceful retreat from Scotland's
largest city just next door.

Facing away from the road, start
at the right-hand side of a car park
on Balgraystone Road, south of
St Luke's High School, on the edge

of Barrhead. Join a track heading
towards Balgray Reservoir, branching
right at a fork after 20m. The track
skims the south edge of the reservoir,
a good place to see great crested
grebes, known for their ornate head
plumage and spectacular courtship
ritual at the start of the breeding
season. This is also the best part of
the walk for a picnic break, either
now or on the return.

At the end of the reservoir carefully
cross a road and turn left along a
track down the side of Brock Burn. At
a junction, turn right with a view of a
weir and waterfall in the trees behind.
Look out for dippers and kingfishers.

The track now skirts along Ryat Linn
Reservoir to its far end, passing below
a railway viaduct to meet a third
reservoir, Waulkmill Glen. Walk to the
very end of this body of water and
turn right, above the dam, for a view
back to the viaduct.

The reservoirs were all built in the
mid-19th century as part of a vital

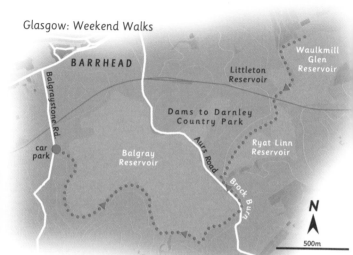

waterworks scheme with a labour force of between 800 and 1000 men, which was designed to meet the demands of Glasgow's fast-growing population. Waulkmill Glen and Ryat Linn were the first to be finished, followed by the larger Balgray Reservoir. The Gorbals Gravitation Water Company ran the works after identifying the Brock Burn as a good source of water.

Beyond Waulkmill Glen Reservoir is where Camp 660, a World War II prisoner of war camp, held Italian and then German servicemen before being put to use in the post-war years for homeless families from Glasgow – it is now part of a residential development.

All three reservoirs are prime birdwatching sites, with many ducks wintering on the water and, in spring, sedge or willow warblers frequenting the area. Look out, too, for common sandpipers on the shoreline. A highlight of summer is the sight of swifts swooping for insects, while autumn sees the return of redwing, fieldfare, wigeon, teal, goldeneye and goosander. You can continue walking below the Waulkmill Glen Reservoir dam but that involves losing height, so the best route back is to retrace your steps to the start.

11

Castle Semple Loch

Distance **8km** Time **2 hours 45**
Terrain **surfaced and unsurfaced paths and tracks, steps**
Map **OS Explorer 341**
Access **regular buses to Lochwinnoch (1km to start of walk) from Johnstone; trains from Glasgow, Ayr and Ardrossan**

Castle Semple Loch is perfect for watersports and the Clyde Muirshiel Regional Park has its own centre here, offering popular water-based courses ranging from paddlesports to sailing. With a shoreline path and woods sweeping up the hillside, it is also a brilliant place for walkers.

From the visitor centre walk down to the loch and turn left along a shore path to some large wooden benches with animal carvings after 1km. Go left up to and across a cycletrack, then through a kissing gate to enter Parkhill Wood. After 300m turn left to cross a footbridge and continue on a surfaced path.

This leads to a pond and grotto, once part of the ornamental grounds of the neoclassical Castle Semple House which replaced the original 16th-century Castle Semple. The house was built in the 18th century for William Macdowall, whose wealth was amassed through Caribbean sugar plantations and the slave trade. After passing through successive generations of Macdowalls, the family's fortunes went into decline and the estate was broken up. The house itself was eventually demolished.

Beyond the grotto go left at a junction and, after 25m, left again onto a path which leads to the top of Park Hill. From here you can look down on the loch and, on a clear day, out to Ailsa Craig, the Firth of Clyde's uninhabited volcanic plug whose granite is one of only two sources of curling stones in the world. The path continues down the other side of the hill, then swings right to a junction. Go straight on, branching left after 40m to walk up along the edge of the wood with great views over the trees.

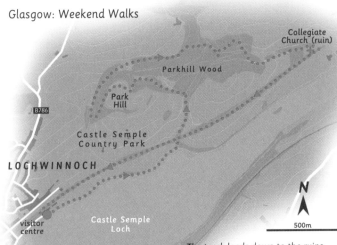

At a fork bear right on the larger of the two paths, down into woodland. After crossing a footbridge go left at a junction to follow a path to the rhododendrons on the hillock of Downies Castle or Mound, which is crowned by ancient yew trees. Cross a very small bridge after the rhododendrons and take the path ahead (rather than to the right). When you meet a track, turn left along it to go through a gate and continue ahead.

The track leads down to the ruins of Castle Semple Collegiate Church, founded at the beginning of the 16th century by John, First Lord Semple, whose tomb is inside. After looking around, carry on down the track until you spot a path to the right just before an old railway bridge. This leads to the cycletrack you crossed earlier.

The cycletrack follows the former Dalry and North Johnstone Railway Line (or the Lochwinnoch Loop as it was known) which closed in the 1960s as part of the Beeching cuts. Turn right to take the cycletrack for just over 2km back to the visitor centre.

12

Clyde Muirshiel Regional Park and Windy Hill

Distance **2km** Time **1 hour 15**
Terrain **surfaced and unsurfaced
paths** Map **OS Explorer 341**
Access **regular buses to
Lochwinnoch (8km to start of
walk) from Johnstone, and trains
from Glasgow, Ayr and Ardrossan**

**At 28,100 hectares (281sq km),
Clyde Muirshiel Regional Park
comprises as much land as some
of the largest Highland estates
and is just as full of fantastic
scenery. From the coast of the
Firth of Clyde to a huge expanse
of inland moorland and hills,
this is a vast area of countryside
just waiting to be explored.**

Deep in the hills above Lochwinnoch
you get a real taste of this part of the
country at the Muirshiel Visitor Centre,
up near the top of Calder Glen. The
volcanic plug of Windy Hill rises above
the visitor centre, a fine little summit
which feels as if it is in the middle of
nowhere, even as you make your

way up a surfaced path. The route
is short and easy, but the views
across the hills to the west and north
are as good as from any higher peak.
On the lower slopes, look out for roe
deer taking advantage of woodland
which is gradually being cleared of
Sitka spruce to allow native species
to establish.

From the far end of the visitor centre
car park, go right and cross an access
road. Follow a path signed for Windy
Hill on the other side and head uphill,
ignoring a turn to the right as you
pass through mixed woodland. At the
top edge of some conifers turn left for
a short section of level ground before
bearing right, up to a gap in an old
drystane dyke. Beyond this the trees
start to thin where downy birch,
rowan and Scots pine have been
planted, encouraging brown hares,
black grouse and butterflies to return
to a hillside which had been
monopolised by invasive spruce and
rhododendron introduced when this

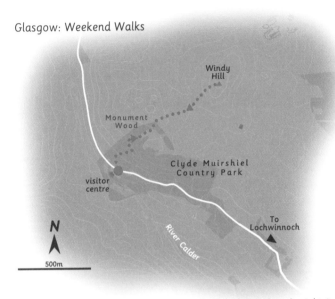

was a Victorian grouse-shooting estate. During the inter-war years, it was one of Scotland's best regarded sporting estates and is said to have been visited by Winston Churchill.

After a metal gate, you emerge onto open moorland and a path runs to the right, along a wall, allowing you to strike out across an empty stretch of high land with Windy Hill ahead. At the end of the surfaced (albeit rather worn-out) path there is a choice of routes to the top. The most direct bears slightly left, up a steep grassy path. The other trail, to the right, is slightly less steep but both lead to the hilltop and its cairn.

After enjoying the views, which also extend east to Glasgow and the Clyde Valley, there really is only one way down that doesn't involve a lot of squelching across boggy ground. So, retrace your steps, with your sightline ranging over the empty rolling moorland ahead as you make your way back on a walk which seems almost disproportionately easy for such a feeling of remoteness.

13

Greenock Cut Nature Trail

Distance 2.5km **Time** 1 hour 15
Terrain surfaced and unsurfaced
paths, steps **Map** OS Explorer 341
Access regular buses to Inverkip
(4.5km to start of walk) from
Glasgow, Greenock and Largs

**The Greenock Cut is a 6.5km
aqueduct built along with the
Great Reservoir (now Loch
Thom) and Compensation
Reservoir in the 1820s, powering
the paper, cotton, woollen,
sugar-refining and shipbuilding
industries to which the town of
Greenock owed its wealth.**

From its inception, the Cut also
offered well-attired Georgians an
elevated promenade from which they
could survey this busy stretch of the
Firth of Clyde as steamboats plied the
waters from Greenock's quay to ports
up and down the west coast. Today its
towpath character, intersected by a
score of small stone bridges, makes
the Cut a less formal but no less
striking vantage point over the river
and the Clyde Muirshiel Regional Park.

Starting from the Greenock Cut
Visitor Centre, head right on the road
and go down a path which begins to
the right of a bridge. Pass a stone
monument to Robert Thom, cottonmill
owner and engineer, who designed
this innovative 'green' power scheme
in the 1820s and after whom the main
reservoir is named. Half a century
earlier, James Watt, arguably
Greenock's most famous son, had
overseen a project to improve the
water supply to the town from two
small reservoirs on Whinhill but by the
1820s this was inadequate.

Drop down to the start of the
Greenock Cut. The 15 months of
labour to dig out this trench on the
edge of the moor would have been
back-breaking, with little opportunity
for labourers to enjoy the view to the
isles in the Firth of Clyde. The Cut was
used until 1971, with the workers who
were employed to break the surface
ice in winter housed in basic bothies.

Cross a bridge over a sluice gate and
turn right (if you are lucky water will
be cascading out of Compensation

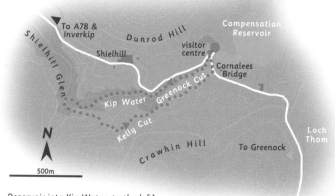

Reservoir into Kip Water, to the left). The path continues between the Cut to the right and the burn down below. After passing through a metal gate take a path on the left, away from the Cut and down steps.

Once through a wooden gate the path descends and you can try to spot the 12 'Wood Spirits', carved wooden faces positioned among the trees by the ranger service. The woodland is home to native hazel, rowan, oak, ash and willow, and resonates to the sound of birdsong, especially during the breeding and fledging frenzy of spring and summer.

When you reach the burn, take the path over a series of small bridges before duckboards lead you along the opposite bank of the usually roaring water. After a gate the boards steer you left to climb steadily to a path, where you turn left and follow a ditch. This is the Kelly Cut, built in 1845, with views down the glen through which the Kip Water makes its brief journey to the Firth of Clyde. In sunshine, dragonflies dart above the water, in spring you may spot cuckoos and skylarks on the moor and, if you are lucky, a hen harrier may even pass overhead.

At a minor road go left to pass the end of Compensation Reservoir and return to the visitor centre.

14

Lang Craigs

Distance **6km** Time **2 hours 45**
Terrain **surfaced and unsurfaced
paths, muddy in places, steps.
Do take care at the top, especially
with children, as the drop from
the crags is severe**
Map **OS Explorer OL38**
Access **regular buses to
Dumbarton Road (2km to start of
walk) from Glasgow city centre**

**In the sheltered glen above
Overtoun House, an ancient
woodland has gained a new
lease of life with younger native
trees planted in the largest
Woodland Trust site in the west
of Scotland. Above all of this,
the rocky outcrops of Lang
Craigs provide a lofty viewpoint
across the Kilpatrick Hills, over
to Loch Lomond and down to
the River Clyde.**

The walk starts outside Overtoun
House, 3km east of Dumbarton and
just under 2km from the A82 at
Milton. Built in 1862 for a wealthy
lawyer, it was used as a convalescent
home for wounded soldiers during
World War II after being given to the
public in 1938.

Go past the main entrance and cross
the Overtoun Bridge over the gorge,
where it's wise to keep dogs on a lead
as some have apparently leapt over
the parapets here. Turn right on the
other side. A path runs up Overtoun
Burn; ignore turnings to the right and
left to reach a footbridge, which you
cross to go past an old fishpond. Turn
left at a path junction, then keep left
once past the pond. Continue by the
burn to cross a wooden footbridge
(not the stone one before it) and turn
right. Re-cross the burn higher up, on
a metal footbridge, and walk up to a
gate in a tall fence. A surfaced path on
the other side continues uphill –
ignore the first grassy path on the left
but take the second. This follows a
fairly straight line below Lang Craigs,
up to the right. Behind, views of the
Clyde open out.

Cross a couple of less distinct paths
and continue up to a bench and then
to the left of a grassy hillock (Round

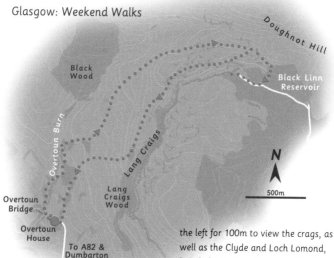

Wood Hill) where a cup-marked stone and other signs of prehistoric habitation have been found. Go straight on at a marker post and ignore steps up to the right. You have now left the waymarked Round Wood Hill Trail, but the path ahead is obvious and offers a taster of the Kilpatrick Hills.

Around 50m before a deer fence, go left, then pass through a gate to leave the Woodland Trust site. After 200m turn right up a path, then right again at a track. At the top follow a fence to the left for 100m to view the crags, as well as the Clyde and Loch Lomond, but do be aware of the very big drops.

Retrace your steps to the junction near the deer fence. Go left here and follow a grassy path for 600m to a marker post, where you turn left again. The path drops and goes through a gap in an old drystane dyke before climbing to the top of a hillock by the southern end of Lang Craigs.

Cross the summit, then walk down steps to the right. At the bottom go straight on at a marker post, then left at a surfaced path. Turn left again at the next two junctions to pass through a metal gate and follow a wide path back to Overtoun House.

15

Balloch Castle Country Park

Distance **4km** Time **1 hour 45**
Terrain **surfaced and unsurfaced
paths, steps** Map **OS Explorer OL38**
Access **regular buses and trains to
Balloch (1.5km to start of walk)
from Glasgow and Dumbarton**

**You couldn't really get a
more tartan and shortbread
setting than Balloch Castle,
the Scottish baronial pile above
Loch Lomond. Locals and
tourists flock here and it is
no wonder, with the former
country estate offering parkland,
woods and more than a slice
of history on the celebrated
bonnie banks.**

Walk to the end of a car park sited
100m north of Balloch Castle, which
was built in 1808 for John Buchanan, a
partner in the Glasgow Ship Bank, and
take a path on the left. At a wider path
go right to pass parkland, ignoring a
left and then a right turning before
dropping through woodland. When the

path bends left, go right (after a low
bench) to drop down a rough path.
Along the way, it turns left to shadow
the secretive little Burn of Balloch on
its journey to Scotland's largest and
most famous freshwater loch.

At the bottom, follow the path to the
left above Loch Lomond's shore where
it's possible to descend to little pebble
beaches. Go right at a junction, past a
playground and a stone boathouse,
then keep straight ahead to the river.

Near here, a mound and ditch is all
that remains of the original 13th-
century castle of the Earls of Lennox,
built on land given to the family in
1072 by Malcolm III, son of Duncan
who was murdered by Macbeth. The
castle was abandoned in around 1390
for a more secure location on the
loch's most southerly and Britain's
largest inland island, Inchmurrin.

Take the main path along the
riverbank. Across the water is Balloch
Pier. In its heyday, the railway line ran
right up to the pier where paddle

steamers like the *Maid of the Loch* conveyed visitors onward for tours of the waters. At a large junction, turn left up a surfaced path lined with lights.

After 300m, turn left via a sign for the walled garden, dating from the 19th century and still well tended, though sadly without the peaches, grapes and artichokes that once grew here among more humble vegetables and fruit used in the castle kitchens. Go right at a junction (or detour left to the garden), then take the next turning on the right. Follow a path uphill and to the left to the next junction, now turning left onto a wide surfaced path.

At a fork, bear left to reach Balloch Castle, then skirt round its left side for loch views. Beyond the castle, go right up stone steps into an ornamental Chinese-inspired garden, which still contains some of the original acers and conifers from the 19th century. Leave the garden on the left before turning right to the car park near the start.

16

Mugdock Country Park

Distance **3.75km** Time **1 hour 30**
Terrain **surfaced paths and tracks,**
steps Map **OS Explorer 348**
Access **regular buses to**
Strathblane (3.8km to start of
walk) from Glasgow

Mugdock Country Park forms
a gateway between the city
lights of Glasgow and the dark
skies of the Southern Highlands.
From the park's northern end
the Campsies present a natural
fortification against the wilder
country beyond, but people don't
just come here for the views:
Mugdock is littered with historic
finds, woven together with a
delightful network of paths.

Start at the entrance to Craigend
Visitor Centre. Just west of here is the
heavily wooded Gallowhill, where
hangings took place until 1718 while
on its slopes the Drowning Pond was
used to determine the guilt of any
unfortunates accused of witchcraft.
After World War II, its slopes were
home to a number of the 2000
animals that formed part of the
short-lived Craigend Zoo.

Head to the far side of the visitor
centre, built as stables at the same
time as Craigend Castle (the first
objective in this walk), at the turn
of the 19th century. Follow a path
straight ahead, through woods and
then down and to the right to reach
the fenced-off ruins of the castle.
The estate was owned by various
members of the Smith family,
including John Smith, West Indies
merchant and later, in 1751, founder
of the booksellers John Smith & Son.

At a junction after the castle, go
right on a path, then swing left before
a meadow. Descend to skim the right
side of the fancifully named Khyber
Field. The adjacent 'Khyber Pass'
has none of the drama of its
celebrated Hindu Kush counterpart
but in the 1930s was a gateway for
holidaymakers trudging the final miles
from Milngavie Station to their huts at
Carbeth whilst a new breed of Glasgow
climber made for the warming embers
of the nearby Craigallan Fire.

63

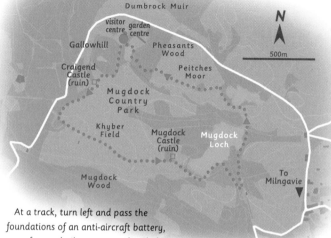

At a track, turn left and pass the
foundations of an anti-aircraft battery,
one of many built to protect the Clyde
during World War II. Carry on through
a gate to reach the 14th-century
Mugdock Castle, once the stronghold
of Clan Graham. In 1945 it was
bought by Hugh Fraser, owner of the
House of Fraser, whose son, Sir Hugh,
gave the estate to the council in 1981
for development into a country park.

Pass the castle on its right to follow
the south shore of Mugdock Loch.
Further round, the path peels away
from the water and leads to a junction:
go left to return to the water. At the
next junction carry straight on up an
unsignposted and initially rocky path.

Go left at a fork, then left again to skirt
above Craigend Quarry. Keep on the
surfaced path as it bends left and
crosses Peitches Moor, named after
Peech Farm which once stood here,
with great views to the Campsies.
Listen out for meadow pipit and curlew.

Dive into the trees at Pheasants
Wood, turn left at a junction and,
after going through a mass of
rhododendrons, turn left again to
walk down steps to Craigend Pond.
Turn right at the water's edge to loop
around the pond, past a garden centre
and up a path to the visitor centre.

17

Duncryne

Distance **2.75km** Time **1 hour 15**
Terrain **minor road, unsurfaced
paths, muddy in places**
Map **OS Explorer OL38**
Access **regular buses to Gartocharn
from Alexandria and Balmaha**

**This is a short walk up a
little hill, but the outlook is
truly world class and should
definitely be saved for a clear
day. Duncryne (or the
Dumpling, as it is known
locally) was a favourite of
Tom Weir, the climber, author
and broadcaster, who used to
live below it. Only when you
reach the top of the volcanic
plug is the view of Loch Lomond
revealed, the backdrop of
mountains arranged as if by
design to make the scene all
the more enchanting.**

From the centre of Gartocharn head
up Duncryne Road to the left of the
House of Darrach, a mix of
womenswear, gifts and a coffee shop.
After 750m go left through a wooden

kissing gate next to a large metal
gate to enter woodland.

Follow the path to the edge of
fields and then through two gates.
A further path, often muddy, leads up
towards Duncryne, between two
fences. Go through another gate at
the end of this path and turn right
before taking a looping trail round to
the left (ignore a path to the right
higher up) to reach the trig point at
the top of the hill.

This is a place to linger – don't rush
back down before savouring the view,
one of the best in all of Scotland.
Weather permitting, take a picnic to
enjoy on the large grassy area at the
top. You are actually standing on all
that remains of a long-extinct
volcano. This plug is hardened
magma and all the other rock has
been eroded over millennia. Looking
over Loch Lomond, you can see
islands ranged along the line of the
Highland Boundary Fault, which
divides the Highlands from the
Lowlands. The loch contains 22
islands and 27 islets in total.

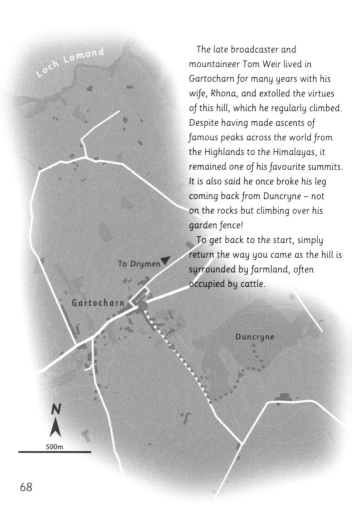

The late broadcaster and mountaineer Tom Weir lived in Gartocharn for many years with his wife, Rhona, and extolled the virtues of this hill, which he regularly climbed. Despite having made ascents of famous peaks across the world from the Highlands to the Himalayas, it remained one of his favourite summits. It is also said he once broke his leg coming back from Duncryne – not on the rocks but climbing over his garden fence!

To get back to the start, simply return the way you came as the hill is surrounded by farmland, often occupied by cattle.

Loch Lomond

To Drymen

Gartocharn

Duncryne

N

500m

18

Earl's Seat

Distance **11km** Time **4 hours 45**
Terrain **hill paths, muddy in
places, tracks** Map **OS Explorer 348**
Access **regular buses to start of
walk from Glasgow**

**Earl's Seat is the highest point
in the Campsie Fells, situated on
a plateau of high ground with
far-reaching views.**

Setting out from near Glengoyne
Distillery, just off the A81 between the
villages of Strathblane and Killearn,
the route passes the dramatic volcanic
plug of Dumgoyne, a possible detour
if your legs are not too tired on what
is the toughest walk in this volume
(but still easily manageable for
anyone of reasonable fitness). There
follows a fine upland tramp amid
spectacularly rugged scenery.

Start 150m north of the distillery.
With an abundance of tumbling
watercourses, the glens of the
Campsies have a long history of
whisky distilling – much of it illicit –
and for many residents these
activities, conducted in farms and

cottages with raw materials secreted
by horseback, was just a way of life.
Burnfoot Farm, where Glengoyne now
stands, was one such illicit still. Even
after it became a legal distillery in
1833, cheating the excisemen by
smuggling from warehouses
continued, until the appointment of
Arthur John Tedder as on-site excise
officer in 1889; he was knighted 20
years later for his 'inestimable
assistance' to stemming the illicit flow
of whisky across the country.

Take a track on the right, signed at
the bottom as a private road. This
becomes rougher after some cottages
and a fork, where you go right.

After passing through a gateway
cross a stone bridge over a burn
and continue up the track and
through a gate on the right into a
field. Bear left, past two arrays of
solar panels, and skirt to the right of
some pines. Cross a couple of tracks
and carry on in the same direction to
the upper end of the field and two
stiles either side of a small burn.

Beyond these, the gradient on the

open hillside increases considerably as you take the left of two paths, climbing the steep grassy slopes below imposing Dumgoyne. Take your time to enjoy the view back to Loch Lomond and the mountains that surround it. When the gradient eases, the hardest part of the route is over and you now contour left around the side of Dumgoyne (save your detour for the return when you'll know if you have any reserves left).

After Dumgoyne, the path widens as it carries on between grassy hillocks. There's a brief section of steeper ground as the route climbs to a cairn just below the top of Garloch Hill. Earl's Seat is now in sight to the east, but it is best to follow a path along the edge of the escarpment to the left and bask in the views northwards to the Trossachs.

Turn left after leaving the top of Garloch Hill and make your descent before tackling Bell Craig. Drop down to a fence and cross this (there is a gate 50m to the right, but it is often locked) before continuing along the escarpment, climbing up another hill, to a cairn.

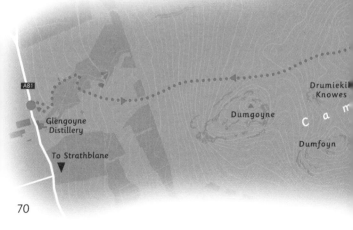

A81

Glengoyne
Distillery

To Strathblane

Drumieki
Knowes

Dumgoyne

c a m

Dumfoyn

Earl's Seat

The path now starts to bear right, dipping down before crossing another hillock and some boggy ground beyond, with peat hags over to the right. Just after these, go right over a final hillock and up to the top of Earl's Seat and its trig point, behind a fence, at 578m.

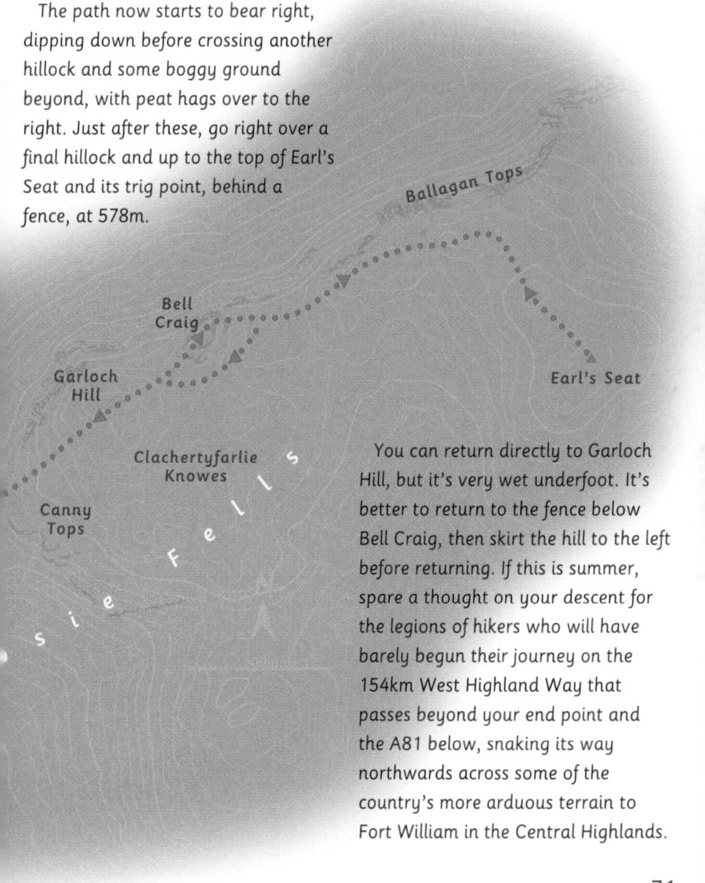

Ballagan Tops

Bell Craig

Garloch Hill

Earl's Seat

Clachertyfarlie Knowes

Canny Tops

s i e   F e l l s

You can return directly to Garloch Hill, but it's very wet underfoot. It's better to return to the fence below Bell Craig, then skirt the hill to the left before returning. If this is summer, spare a thought on your descent for the legions of hikers who will have barely begun their journey on the 154km West Highland Way that passes beyond your end point and the A81 below, snaking its way northwards across some of the country's more arduous terrain to Fort William in the Central Highlands.

19

Campsie Glen

Distance **2.5km** Time **1 hour 15**
Terrain **surfaced and unsurfaced
paths, steps** Map **OS Explorer 348**
Access **regular buses to Clachan of
Campsie from Glasgow**

**Campsie Glen, tucked below
the hills of the same name,
is a great short walk with a
sense of adventure as you round
corners to encounter waterfalls
and gain height for exhilarating
airy views.**

The picturesque gorge carrying the
Kirk Burn became a popular
destination for urban dwellers in the
19th century when a railway linking
Glasgow with Aberfoyle was built,
allowing easy access to the
countryside to the north of the city.

This route begins at Clachan of
Campsie but before starting out it's
worth heading left at the top of the
square to see the ruins of St Machan's
Church. The 12th-century missionary
is thought to have been buried here
after building a chapel on the spot,
while the village itself was a focal

point of the area until Lennoxtown –
known then as Newton of Campsie –
was built in the 18th century. In the
graveyard stands the mausoleum of
the powerful Lennox family, as well as
the grave of one John Bell, physician
to Peter the Great.

After looking round the kirk and its
cemetery, walk to the right of some
buildings and then turn left up a
surfaced path. Go straight ahead at
an information panel, staying on the
surfaced path to admire the waterfalls
as you make your way up the burn.
To the left was a bleachfield which
employed around 50 people in the
mid-19th century, when the village
was a thriving hub of 28 households.

The path ends at a barrier at James'
Linn waterfall, beyond which it's not
safe to go any further. Retrace your
steps to the junction at the
information panel and turn left, where
a steep muddy path leads up the
wooded slopes of the glen. After
500m the gradient eases and you leave the
trees behind. The main path then
swings up to the right but this walk

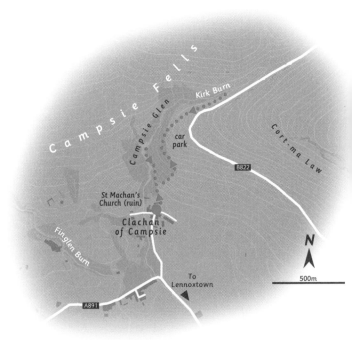

continues straight on, through bracken. (For a detour, you can go right to a car park by the B822 Crow Road, known locally as 'The Car Park in the Sky'. There's a good view here, looking along the escarpment of the Campsies lined with layers of 300-million-year-old lava.)

Once you are through the bracken keep left to make your way down steps and reach some impressive waterfalls, but take care as the drops are severe and exposed. Weather permitting, this is a grand spot for a picnic before retracing your steps down to the start.

20

Dungoil in the Campsies

Distance **7.5km** Time **2 hours 45**
Terrain **forest tracks and hill paths, some steep**
Map **OS Explorer 348**
Access **no public transport to the start; take care not to block access to gates when parking**

The B822 Crow Road is a fantastic stretch of tarmac between Fintry and Lennoxtown, climbing high up through the Campsie Fells. To the west is Dungoil, a prominent and isolated hill offering superb views across the range and north to the Trossachs. The walk to its summit is relatively short but it feels much further removed from the Central Belt than it actually is.

Start at grid reference NS641850 and go over a stile to the right of a farm gate on the west side of the Crow Road. A track on the other side of the gate leads across a large field, often containing sheep – keep dogs on a lead. The face of Dungoil looming

above you at this point presents a fearsome prospect, but don't worry, this route takes you up more gentle slopes on the other side.

After 700m go through a gate on the edge of forestry and continue ahead. Another 1.8km further on, after the track has bent round to the left, keep left at a junction. Look for roe deer as you make your way through the forestry. At another junction, where the main track goes up to the right, go left downhill.

Once past an area of boggy ground to the right, the track rises and bears right. Go left after the track levels out (just before it begins to dip) and pick your way through trees on a faint, steep trail which leads to the edge of the forestry. Bear right to clamber up a short but very steep grass and rock slope and emerge out of the silence of the trees onto open hillside. Keep an eye out for buzzards hunting around here and listen for their mournful call.

A grass path, boggy in places, then curves round to the right to the two summits of Dungoil. Like many of the isolated peaks that stand out so prominently in the wider area, Dungoil is volcanic. It is one of a number of vents in the Clyde Plateau and the largest of its kind in the Campsie Fells. Of the two summits, the one furthest away is the high point – from it you can see where you started the walk far below. The views across this volcanic landscape are extensive and include the Campsie Fells and Fintry and Gargunnock Hills, as well as the more distant Trossachs.

Linger on the summit for as long as you can as this is one of the loveliest hilltops in Scotland and you may well have it to yourself, such is the (mistaken) rush by many to head for higher mountains to the north.

Return the same way you came as the more direct route back to the road is steep and extremely hazardous.

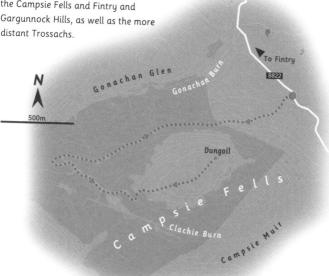

21

Bar Hill

Distance **6km** Time **2 hours 30**
Terrain **surfaced and unsurfaced**
paths and tracks, towpath
Map **OS Explorer 348**
Access **buses to Auchinstarry from**
Croy, Camelon and Cumbernauld

The northwest frontier of the
Roman Empire might sound
like the title of a Hollywood
blockbuster but it is actually
a real thing, in existence today
and there to be explored.

The Antonine Wall stretched for
60km across Scotland, from the Firth of
Clyde to the Firth of Forth – the most
complex frontier ever built by the
Roman Army yet only occupied for
about 20 years. Now a World Heritage
Site, one of the best sections lies just
south of Kilsyth on Bar Hill where the
highest of its series of forts (set,
unusually, apart from the wall) once
stood. This walk climbs to the turf and
earth ramparts, built on a bed of stone
under the orders of Emperor Antoninus
Pius in 142AD, with sweeping views
across to the Campsies and Kilsyth Hills.

Start at Auchinstarry Marina, a
mooring basin for narrowboats on
the Forth & Clyde Canal. Opened in
1790, the canal was the biggest
infrastructure project in Scotland after
the Antonine Wall, which it roughly
follows, allowing seaborne craft to
travel the breadth of Scotland from the
Forth to the Clyde. Like the wall, its
useful life was brief – even before the
advent of the railways a move towards
larger seagoing vessels meant it was
too narrow for its original purpose.

Head to the west end of the basin
car park. A sign points left up a path
which runs to the right of a sensory
garden, then up and over a hill
beyond. Some 50m after the path
begins to lose height, go right on a
grassy trail to meet a road. Cross this
to take a track on the other side,
signed for Bar Hill. You are now on the
John Muir Way, which stretches for
215km from Helensburgh to Dunbar.

Follow the track for 600m, ignoring
turnings to the left, to reach Barhill
Wood, which you enter. At a sign for
Bar Hill, leave the track and go right

81

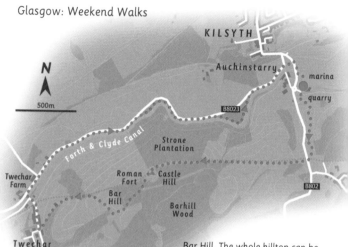

KILSYTH

Auchinstarry

marina

quarry

B8023

Forth & Clyde Canal

Strone
Plantation

Roman   Castle
Fort   Hill

Twechar
Farm

Bar
Hill

Barhill
Wood

B802

Twechar

N

500m

on a wide grassy path to reach an information sign. Beyond this is the huge ditch of the Antonine Wall, leading steeply uphill to the left. Follow the left side of it into a dip and then all the way up the steep slope before bearing left to a trig point on top of Castle Hill, the site of an Iron Age hillfort also used by the Romans.

Cross the hilltop and drop down a steep bank to an information panel, then bear left into trees. Turn left at a fork, then right at a John Muir Way sign to emerge on the grassy top of

Bar Hill. The whole hilltop can be explored, including the site of a bathhouse to the right where soldiers would have relaxed and socialised in steam rooms and saunas. Go over the hill and down to the left to a gate.

A track leads to a second gate; beyond this turn right to walk alongside a large field and down to the left. Ignore a right turn lower down and pass a farmhouse before coming to Twechar. Turn right at a road, beside a war memorial, and continue for 300m to reach the canal. Go right on the other side to follow the towpath for 2.7km, crossing the canal at a roadbridge to the start.

22

Chatelherault Country Park

Distance **8km** Time **2 hours 45**
Terrain **surfaced and unsurfaced paths and tracks, steps**
Map **OS Explorer 343**
Access **regular buses to the main entrance to the country park (650m to start of walk) from Hamilton; trains to Chatelherault Station (800m to start of walk) from Glasgow**

When Chatelherault was built as a hunting lodge for the 5th Duke of Hamilton by William Adam in the mid-18th century, it was a place for the landed gentry to enjoy the scenery and shoot. The name is derived from the title Duc de Châtellerault, which the duke also held. At the heart of the country park lies the Avon Water gorge where the ancient Cadzow Oaks can be found.

To start the walk, go left at the information board as you face Chatelherault's former hunting lodge (now the visitor centre). After 10m turn left again to follow a wide path which swings round to the right and enters woodland. Continue on this path for another 1.75km to a junction, then go left to reach Green Bridge at the bottom of steps after a further 1.5km. This first section passes through woodland filled with birdsong where a bench at the junction is a good place to pause and listen.

Cross Green Bridge (which is not actually green), then head up and to the right, back into woodland. Ignore steps on the left and continue steeply up to rise high above the river once more. Carry on for 1.7km beyond Green Bridge, ignoring two paths to the right before turning right 150m further on, down a path which crosses Divoty Glen, an enchanting shady dell.

Turn right on meeting a track and follow it to the Cadzow Oaks and Earthworks on the left. Some of these gloriously gnarled and moss-hung trees are over 500 years old and the

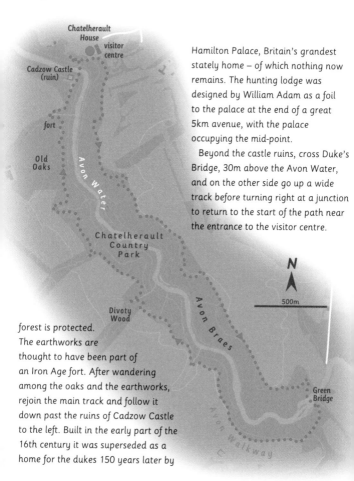

Chatelherault
House

visitor
centre

Cadzow Castle
(ruin)

fort

Old
Oaks

Avon Water

Chatelherault
Country
Park

Divoty
Wood

N

500m

Avon Braes

Green
Bridge

Avon Walkway

Hamilton Palace, Britain's grandest stately home – of which nothing now remains. The hunting lodge was designed by William Adam as a foil to the palace at the end of a great 5km avenue, with the palace occupying the mid-point.

Beyond the castle ruins, cross Duke's Bridge, 30m above the Avon Water, and on the other side go up a wide track before turning right at a junction to return to the start of the path near the entrance to the visitor centre.

forest is protected. The earthworks are thought to have been part of an Iron Age fort. After wandering among the oaks and the earthworks, rejoin the main track and follow it down past the ruins of Cadzow Castle to the left. Built in the early part of the 16th century it was superseded as a home for the dukes 150 years later by

23

Strathclyde Country Park

Distance **6.5km** Time **1 hour 30**
Terrain **surfaced paths**
Map **OS Explorer 343**
Access **regular buses to the
A723 at the south end of the
country park (400m to start of
walk) from Motherwell, Hamilton
and Glasgow**

**Strathclyde Country Park was
built in the 1970s on the site of
Bothwellhaugh, a derelict
former mining village. Since
then, this 400-hectare park has
become a popular destination
for everyone from dog walkers
to international-class athletes,
thrill seekers to history lovers.
This walk is straightforward
with little chance of getting lost
and lots of places to stop for a
picnic by the man-made loch.**

The park hosted the triathlon event
at the 2014 Commonwealth Games,
as well as rowing when the games
were held in Scotland in 1986. On
weekends around the year, rowers
and sailors are often on the water,
while joggers and cyclists make use of
the good paths around the edge.
Despite all this activity, and the M74
to the west, the water and woodland
offer a good nesting site for birds.

The walk starts at the south end of
the loch. Head towards the brick-built
watersports centre on an obvious
path. With the River Clyde over to
your left, stay by the loch all the way
to the far end, where you cross an
access road and follow a path away
from the water up to the right. Keep
going right, through a small wood, to
rejoin the loch shore. To the left is a
theme park, more suited to those out
for an adrenaline rush than a gentle
stroll. The mix of razzmatazz and
country park here is not new: in 1994
this was the location of the first ever
T in the Park music festival, with
performances from Blur and Oasis.

A century and a half earlier, this
was the Low Parks of Hamilton
Palace, but the discovery in 1850 of
extensive coal seams on the estate led
to pits being sunk for what became
the Hamilton Palace Colliery – it was

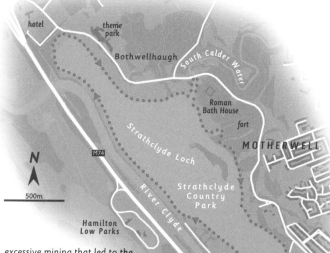

hotel

theme park

Bothwellhaugh

South Calder Water

Roman Bath House

fort

MOTHERWELL

Strathclyde Loch

N

M74

500m

River Clyde

Strathclyde Country Park

Hamilton Low Parks

excessive mining that led to the ultimate demolition of the palace in the 1920s. Forty years later, the pit had closed and the miners' village, known as 'The Pallis', with its 450 homes, two schools and two kirks, was derelict.

After passing a large car park follow a path left, away from the loch, taking the second right in 100m. Cross a footbridge over the South Calder Water, then go right to pass the ruins of a Roman bath house. Excavated in 1975 in an area now submerged beneath Strathclyde Loch, and then moved here, it was in use in the 2nd century by a garrison of 500 soldiers stationed at a nearby fort around a day's march from the Antonine Wall.

Go straight on at the junction, then turn right at the next one to pass through a swathe of woodland. Keep right at all forks to emerge near a sandy beach. The surfaced path leads back to the start.

24

New Lanark and the Falls of Clyde

Distance **11.5km** Time **3 hours 45 minutes** Terrain **surfaced and unsurfaced paths, steps** Map **OS Explorer 335** Access **regular buses to New Lanark from Glasgow via Lanark**

In the 1800s, New Lanark was home to an industrial experiment which paved the way for social reformers the world over. Upstream from the mills and stone-built 'high rises' that comprise this World Heritage Site where at its peak 2000 people lived or worked, the Falls of Clyde now power another industry: hydro-electricity. It is the overarching beauty of the waterfalls, however, that is the biggest draw for walkers.

With its stone tenements nestling at the base of a deep chasm through which the tumultuous whitewater of the Clyde rages, such is the preserved integrity of this mill village that as you descend into the gorge – invariably on foot (as parking is located above) – you could be stepping back more than two centuries to when Glasgow banker and entrepreneur David Dale first brought his celebrated industrial powerhouse into being in 1785.

Within a decade, Dale's cotton mills had become the biggest single industrial enterprise in Scotland, but it was Dale's experiments in education and community provision that began to attract as many observers as his revolutionary mechanical processes. Like many industrialists, he relied largely on a labour force of nimble-fingered orphans (800 of the 1100 workers were children), but made sure they were well-clothed and fed and provided with two hours of schooling daily, truly revolutionary for the age.

When, in 1800, Dale sold New Lanark to his son-in-law Robert Owen, an ambitious Welsh social reformer, the experiment reached a new pitch – Owen raised the minimum age for millworkers from six to 12, started

what was
likely to be the
industrial world's
first on-site crèche and
opened an institution
through which children
learnt to dance, play
music and sing.

Such was the success of
the enterprise and its impact
on social reformers and
educationalists internationally
that Robert Owen was lured
away to the New World to set up
a similar enterprise in 1824. The
New Lanark community continued
unabated, diversifying into ropeworks,
but when this closed in 1967 the
buildings were threatened with
demolition. Thankfully, conservation
bodies stepped in and it was restored
to become one of Scotland's most
visited tourist attractions.

From the centre of New Lanark go
through a set of large metal gates in
front of the mill complex, then down
steps to the right of the visitor centre.
At the bottom head left to reach the
Scottish Wildlife Trust's visitor centre for

the Falls of Clyde. Continue left up steps opposite, then turn right to begin the walk by the Clyde. Ignore turnings to the left as you make your way along the river. At a fork keep right to follow a boardwalk before joining a track which passes a house and goes on to a junction at the hydro-electric power station, where you go right.

A steep path runs up past two very large water pipes to a viewing area over the falls of Corra Linn. Above this are the ruins of Bonnington Pavilion, or the Hall of Mirrors, dated 1708. Designed as an immersive experience for distinguished visitors to the long-gone Bonnington House, the mirrors were intended to create the illusion that the viewer was standing in the midst of Corra Linn.

The route goes up six steps which begin just to the left of the viewing area, then right to follow a sign for Bonnington Linn. Keep on the main path until you come to a bridge; cross the water here, turning right on the other side to follow a track for 150m before going right again down a path.

Enjoy views of Bonnington Linn before continuing high above the river, ignoring steps to the left.

At a field, the path leads past the ruins of the 16th-century Corra Castle and down to some good viewpoints next to Corra Linn. Continue down to the riverside before rising again and going right at a fork. When the path leaves the river, turn right at a track which leads to a road in front of flats. Go right to reach the bottom of the road, then right again to cross the Clyde via a stone bridge.

On the other side head right, through a metal gate and down a lane to pass through a gate on the left. Take a grassy riverside path past the entrance to a water treatment plant, then uphill to join the end of a road. Follow the road for 400m to a Clyde Walkway sign pointing down the third driveway on the right; follow this for 100m to a path on the right which returns to the riverside via a series of looping zigzags. After 500m, climb steps, then cross a small bridge before more zigzags rise up to a road. Go right to drop back down to New Lanark.

Tinto

Distance **7km** Time **3 hours**
Terrain **hill paths**
Map **OS Explorer 335**
Access **regular buses along the A73 near Thankerton (350m to start of walk) from Lanark and Biggar**

Tinto is an iconic hill with a proper pointy summit visible to anyone travelling from the south to Glasgow. The views from the top are superb – taking in the Highlands, the Lake District and even the Mountains of Mourne on a clear day.

The first known people to have walked up Tinto lived in the Bronze Age and built a huge cairn at the top which is still there today, 3500 years later. Then, 2000 years ago a pre-Roman hillfort – Fallburn – was built below the slopes (next to the path, 500m from the start). Some also say the name Tinto, meaning 'Hill of Fire', comes from Druidic fires which were once lit to their sun god, Baal.

Whatever mysteries it holds, this is one of the most popular hill climbs in the south of Scotland and it is without a doubt the perfect first hill for children.

Start at the walkers' car park 350m from the A73 and the Tinto Hill Tearoom near Thankerton. Go through a gate at the top of the car park, by an information board. Higher up pass through a kissing gate and walk below electricity wires – Fallburn Hillfort is to the left at this point and the ditches which encircle it can be made out below four concentric ramparts which were once much higher.

Continue on the path as it rises up the right side of Totherin Hill, which obscures the view of Tinto. After the path has swung fairly sharply to the left, pass the cairn at the top of the main hill's outlier, to your left. At just over halfway, this is a good place for a rest before continuing up the wide path. At a junction go left – another path goes straight on, above the dramatic corrie of Maurice's Cleuch, but it is eroded in parts.

The main path runs up and to the right before reaching the final steep

To Lanark Tearoom

A73

car park

fort

Westbank Plantation

Maurice's Cleuch

Totherin Hill

Tinto Hills

N

500m

Tinto

pull to the huge Bronze Age cairn (and viewfinder compass) at the top – at over 6m high, one of the biggest in Scotland. The trig point is below the cairn, on the other side of a fence.

Stone shelters around the base of the cairn make good picnic spots and on a clear day the views from the 707m summit are worth lingering for. Skiddaw in the Lake District and the Mountains of Mourne in Northern Ireland can be seen, as well as the nearer Isle of Arran, the Trossachs and, to the east, the Pentlands.

The best route of return is to retrace your steps, taking time to enjoy the panorama on the way down. Look out, too, for wildlife – golden plover and ring ouzel on the upper slopes, hen harrier or merlin hunting over the heather moors, as well as lapwing, curlew, skylark and snipe.

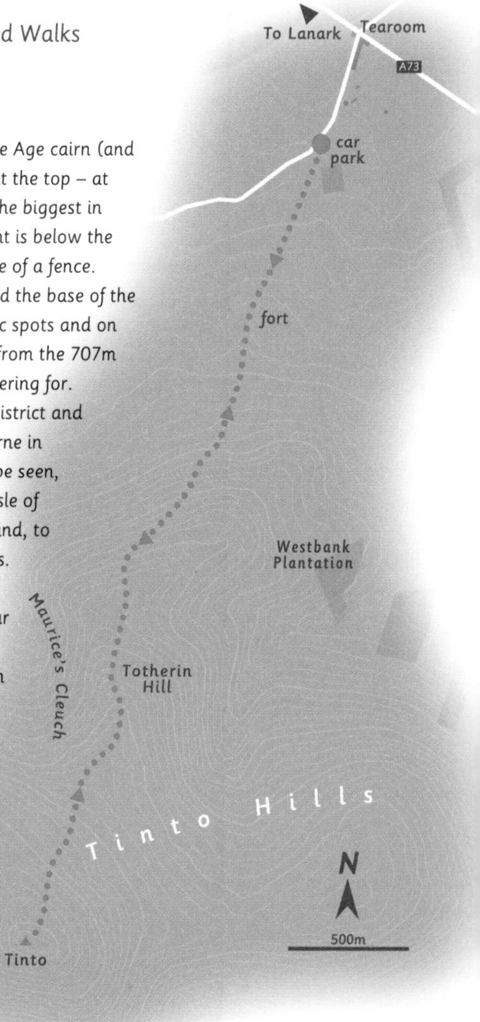